C000024815

Historic, archived document

Do not assume content reflects current
scientific knowledge, policies, or practices.

ISBN 978-1-5281-2578-9
PIBN 10898602

English
Français
Deutsche
Italiano
Español
Português

www.forgottenbooks.com

Mythology Photography **Fiction**
Fishing Christianity **Art** Cooking
Essays Buddhism Freemasonry
Medicine **Biology** Music **Ancient**
Egypt Evolution Carpentry Physics
Dance Geology **Mathematics** Fitness
Shakespeare **Folklore** Yoga Marketing
Confidence Immortality Biographies
Poetry **Psychology** Witchcraft
Electronics Chemistry History **Law**
Accounting **Philosophy** Anthropology
Alchemy Drama Quantum Mechanics
Atheism Sexual Health **Ancient History**
Entrepreneurship Languages Sport
Paleontology Needlework Islam
Metaphysics Investment Archaeology
Parenting Statistics Criminology
Motivational

Moisture Use by Various Plant Species and its Relation to Pan Evaporation and Net Radiation

August 1965   **ARS 41-112**
Agricultural Research Service
UNITED STATES DEPARTMENT OF AGRICULTURE

CONTENTS

Moisture Use by Various Plant Species and its Relation to Pan Evaporation and Net Radiation[1]

B. D. Doss, O. L. Bennett, and D. A. Ashley,
Soil and Water Conservation Research Division

INTRODUCTION

Moisture use by growing plants is governed primarily by the supply of radiant energy when there is an ample supply of soil moisture and a good vegetative cover. With a limited supply of water, the rate of moisture use is principally a function of the amount of water in the soil. As the soil moisture supply decreases, water absorption by the root decreases. Root distribution of plants is important, for it is by root proliferation that much of the soil moisture supply becomes accessible to the plant. For this reason, soil structure, texture, depth, compaction, pH, and other factors affecting root growth are important factors affecting moisture use. Rate of moisture use is governed by vegetative cover only when it is limiting. Once there is complete cover, the rate is dependent on energy supply and available moisture.

Proper scheduling of irrigation applications for optimum yield must be based on information on rate of evapotranspiration and moisture level needed by specific crops at specific stages of growth. Several empirical methods have been developed for estimating evapotranspiration under conditions of high soil moisture using available climatic data (4,15,16).[2] When the water supply is ample, moisture use by a crop approaches a maximum value that depends primarily on climate (16). Relations between moisture use by crops and free-water evaporation have been established for conditions when the soil was irrigated or adequately supplied with moisture (1,3,14). Penman (14) calculated that under a given set of climatic conditions the water use by sod crops under conditions of adequately supplied water was 80 percent of the free-water loss from a specific type of pan during the period May to August. Jensen and coworkers (12) found that over several seasons in central Washington the average relation between evapotranspiration and pan evaporation became relatively constant as soon as the crop foliage completely covered the ground and this relation continued until the crop approached maturity or until harvesting. Doss, Bennett, and Ashley (6) and Fritschen and Shaw (8) each presented a relation between evapotranspiration by corn and pan evaporation that could be used for determining irrigation requirements.

The relation of evapotranspiration to net radiation (ET/Rn) has been reported for several crops (9,10,11,13). Graham and King (10) reported that under Iowa climatic conditions evapotranspiration by corn was controlled by the available energy supply when the soil surface was moist and water was adequately supplied. They found that the ratio of ET/Rn averaged 0.81 ± 0.09

---

[1] In cooperation with the Agronomy and Soils Department, Auburn University Agricultural Experiment Station.
[2] Underscored numbers in parentheses refer to Literature Cited at end of report.

for the daytime period on days following rain when a large area was equally moist. Gerber and Decker in Missouri (9) and Halstead in Maryland (11) showed that lower $\overline{ET}$/Rn ratios occurred when the soil was dry than when wet. The ratio of $\overline{ET}$/Rn for a grass cover under conditions of limited soil moisture was less than 1.0 (11). Lemon and coworkers showed that for irrigated conditions in Texas, the ratio was more than 1.0, because of convective heat transfer from the atmosphere to the crop (13).

EXPERIMENTAL PROCEDURE

Rates of moisture use by 15 different species--cotton (Gossypium hirsutum), Sart sorghum (Sorghum vulgare), corn (Zea mays), bahiagrass (Paspalum notatum), Coastal and common bermudagrass (Cynodon dactylon), dallisgrass (Paspalum dilatatum), sericea lespedeza (Lespedeza cuneata), Atlantic alfalfa (Medicago sativa), intermediate white clover (Trifolium repens), California Ladino clover (Trifolium repens var. Ladino), Kenland red clover (Trifolium pratense), reed canarygrass (Phalaris arundinacea), tall fescue (Festuca arundinacea), and orchardgrass (Dactylis glomerata)--were measured during two or more growing seasons from 1956 to 1962 at Thorsby, Ala. These rates were determined from 2 to 4 gravimetric soil samples per plot taken at 3- to 5-day intervals to a depth of 48 inches by 6-inch increments with a 3/4-inch tube-type sampler. Sampling started 2 or 3 days after rainfall or irrigation water was applied. Daily moisture-use rates were computed from the differences in soil moisture at the beginning and ending of each period. Due allowance was made for additions of moisture from rainfall and irrigation and losses from runoff and deep percolation. Percolation losses were estimated from water added that made the soil moisture in the profile exceed field capacity. Field capacity was determined under field conditions by saturating undisturbed soil, then sampling the soil at daily intervals until drainage practically ceased. Usually little runoff or deep percolation occurred during the period April to October except when rainfall occurred in successive storms or shortly after irrigation.

Moisture use was determined at three different soil moisture regimes for all species except Coastal bermudagrass, which had four regimes, and corn, where only one regime was used. The four soil moisture regimes included no irrigation (M_0) and irrigations when the depletion of available moisture in the rooting zone was 85 percent (M_1); 60 percent for corn, 80 percent for cotton and sorghum, 65 percent for other species (M_2); and 30 percent (M_3), respectively.

The M_1 plots were covered with clear polyethylene during rains except when rainfall occurred at time irrigation was scheduled. All species except cotton were irrigated by a sprinkler system. Cotton was irrigated by the furrow method. Enough water was applied at each irrigation to restore the rooting zone to field capacity.

The plots for all species except the crops to be cultivated and Coastal bermudagrass and alfalfa in 1961 and 1962 were 25 by 40 feet and contained 3 subplots, 6 by 6 feet, for moisture variables. Subplots were spaced 6 feet apart. Each moisture plot was enclosed by a metal frame extending 8 inches into the soil and protruding 2 inches above the ground level to confine water. Plots for crops to be cultivated were 33 by 45 feet or larger. Plots for Coastal bermudagrass and alfalfa in 1961-62 were 24 by 48 feet. All species treatments contained 4 replications.

Rooting depths used to determine when to irrigate were 36 inches for alfalfa and red clover, 30 inches for canarygrass and fescue, and 24 inches for all other species. Rooting depths were determined by measuring soil moisture extraction patterns for each species by sampling the soil to a depth of 48 inches during dry periods.

The soil was a Greenville fine sandy loam. Bulk density values determined from soil samples taken at 3-inch intervals to a depth of 36 inches ranged from 1.60 to 1.65, with an average value of 1.61. The average available water per foot of soil as determined gravimetrically under field conditions was 1.2 inches. Soil fertility was maintained at a high level on all treatments.

Rainfall was measured with a standard U.S. Weather Bureau gage and pan evaporation with a standard U.S. Weather Bureau evaporation pan. Net radiation was measured with a Beckman

Model B radiometer[2] over a mixture of Coastal bermudagrass, fescue, and white clover sod. Rainfall, pan evaporation, and net radiation were measured at a location within the experimental area.

RESULTS AND DISCUSSION

Climatic Data

Rainfall, pan evaporation, net radiation, and mean air temperature by 10-day periods throughout the growing season for each year of record are given in tables 1, 2, 3, and 4, respectively. Average rainfall, pan evaporation, net radiation, and mean air temperature values for all years are shown in figure 1, along with the average moisture use rate curve throughout the

TABLE 1.--Rainfall by 10-day periods throughout growing season for each year, 1956-62

Period		Year							Average	Normal
		1956	1957	1958	1959	1960	1961	1962		
				Inches per 10-day period						
Feb.	11-20	--	0.70	--	--	--	--	--	--	--
	21-28	--	1.21	--	--	--	--	--	--	--
March	1-10	--	.97	--	--	--	--	--	--	--
	11-20	--	.34	--	--	--	--	--	--	--
	21-31	2.22	6.89	1.05	2.94	2.44	4.35	1.98	3.12	2.18
April	1-10	3.12	5.12	.89	.58	1.34	.99	1.73	1.97	1.98
	11-20	2.47	1.34	.79	2.10	.64	1.78	3.76	1.84	1.98
	21-30	0	.19	1.39	.74	.15	.41	1.58	.64	1.98
May	1-10	2.22	2.20	1.35	0.	1.71	.82	.16	1.21	1.34
	11-20	0	3.00	.32	2.04	0	.21	0	.80	1.34
	21-31	1.62	.86	0	5.84	1.05	.73	.31	1.49	1.34
June	1-10	0	.11	1.59	1.47	1.27	.15	0	.66	1.44
	11-20	.87	.08	2.14	.46	.34	3.78	2.07	1.39	1.44
	21-30	.20	5.31	3.48	.58	.90	3.73	.95	2.16	1.44
July	1-10	1.35	.71	3.41	1.77	.79	.53	2.45	1.57	1.98
	11-20	.73	1.74	2.58	1.90	.99	1.16	1.30	1.48	1.98
	21-31	.36	.36	3.74	.19	3.11	1.42	.55	1.39	1.98
Aug.	1-10	2.01	.90	.06	.55	.48	1.65	1.77	1.06	1.73
	11-20	.45	2.20	1.67	.21	1.31	0	.38	.89	1.73
	21-31	1.16	0	1.42	1.97	1.27	2.69	.82	1.33	1.73
Sept.	1-10	1.52	.57	0	2.87	.25	1.24	1.21	1.09	.93
	11-20	.62	1.34	2.75	1.15	1.83	.36	2.14	1.46	.93
	21-30	3.11	3.65	3.71	.92	1.25	0	.09	1.82	.93
Oct.	1-10	1.02	.38	.18	1.18	2.97	.50	.95	1.03	.66
	11-20	0	.30	.08	2.29	.36	0	0	.43	.66
	21-31	2.35	.41	1.00	1.18	.67	0	.29	.84	.66

[2]Trade names and company names are included for the benefit of the reader and do not imply any endorsement or preferential treatment of the product listed by the U.S. Dept. of Agriculture.

3

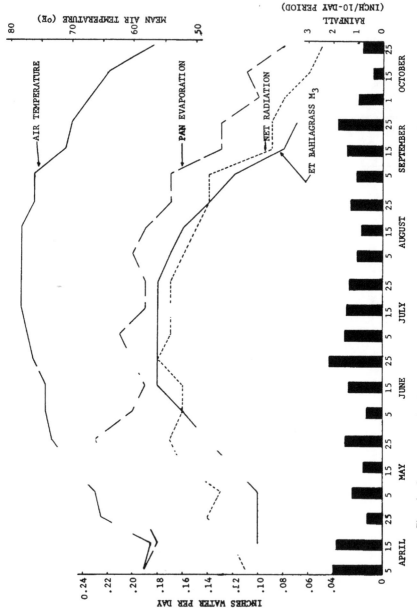

Figure 1.—Open pan evaporation (E), net radiation (Rn), moisture use by bahiagrass M₃ (ET), mean air temperature and rainfall during growing season.

4

TABLE 2.--Average daily rates of open pan evaporation by 10-day periods throughout growing
season for each year, 1956-62

Period		Year							Average
		1956	1957	1958	1959	1960	1961	1962	
				Inches per day					
Feb.	11-20	--	0.11	--	--	--	--	--	--
	21-28	--	.10	--	--	--	--	--	--
March	1-10	--	.07	--	--	--	--	--	--
	11-20	--	.13	--	--	--	--	--	--
	21-31	0.18	.14	0.11	0.17	0.18	--	0.15	0.16
April	1-10	.21	.20	.17	.23	.20	.15	.18	.19
	11-20	.20	.14	.17	.13	.22	.22	--	.18
	21-30	.17	.18	.17	.17	.23	.22	.17	.19
May	1-10	.16	.17	.18	.24	.17	.25	.26	.20
	11-20	.26	.17	.20	.20	.24	.17	.27	.22
	21-31	.20	.22	.25	.21	.24	.22	.26	.23
June	1-10	.24	.20	.24	.12	.19	.21	.19	.20
	11-20	.17	.24	.18	.18	.24	.10	.19	.19
	21-30	.25	.23	.17	.22	.21	.14	.17	.20
July	1-10	.20	.25	.21	.19	.22	.19	.22	.21
	11-20	.25	.23	.15	.16	.19	.14	.24	.19
	21-31	.21	.20	.14	.20	.18	.18	.20	.19
Aug.	1-10	.26	.27	.20	.19	.16	.15	.19	.20
	11-20	.23	.23	.18	.20	.12	.21	.18	.19
	21-31	.17	.22	.16	.19	.16	.14	.18	.17
Sept.	1-10	.18	.17	.19	.14	.18	.16	.16	.17
	11-20	.17	.10	.11	.08	.15	.14	.16	.13
	21-30	.15	.10	.12	.13	.11	.14	.14	.13
Oct.	1-10	.14	.10	.06	.11	.08	.12	.10	.10
	11-20	.11	.12	.14	.09	.08	.15	.11	.11
	21-31	.07	.07	.12	.06	.06	.11	.09	.08

growing season for bahiagrass grown at the M_3 regime. This shows the similarity in seasonal trends of average moisture use by bahiagrass and in climatic factors.

The normal rainfall for the growing season (April - October) is about 30 inches. Rainfall was about 83 percent of normal in 1956, 102 percent in 1957, 108 percent in 1958, 99 percent in 1959, 75 percent in 1960, 73 percent in 1961, and 75 percent in 1962.

TABLE 3.--Average daily rates of net radiation, assuming a constant value for heat of vaporization, by 10-day periods throughout growing season for each year, 1957-62[1]

Period	Year						Average
	1957	1958	1959	1960	1961	1962	
	Inches per day						
March 21-31	0.10	0.07	0.11	0.09	0.08	0.08	0.09
April 1-10	.10	.08	.15	.11	.11	.12	.11
11-20	.09	.12	.10	.15	.16	.12	.12
21-30	.11	.13	.14	.15	.16	.12	.14
May 1-10	.11	.07	.17	.14	.14	.17	.13
11-20	.16	.14	.14	.19	.16	.15	.16
21-31	.19	.18	.15	.19	.16	.13	.17
June 1-10	.15	.19	.11	.17	.18	.14	.16
11-20	.20	.15	.19	.19	.09	.16	.16
21-30	.17	.19	.21	.16	.16	.17	.18
July 1-10	.21	.14	.17	.19	.16	.17	.17
11-20	.20	.14	.17	.17	.14	.18	.17
21-31	.18	.10	.20	.17	.20	.15	.17
Aug. 1-10	.18	.17	--	.15	.14	.17	.16
11-20	.16	.16	--	.14	.16	.15	.15
21-31	.15	.17	.15	.13	.11	.16	.14
Sept. 1-10	.15	.15	.12	.14	.13	.13	.14
11-20	.03	.12	.05	.11	.11	.11	.09
21-30	.04	.10	.09	.07	.13	.10	.09
Oct. 1-10	.05	.08	.07	.08	.08	.10	.08
11-20	.05	.08	.04	.07	.07	--	.06
21-31	.03	.08	.02	.06	.04	.05	.05

[1] Measured over a mixture of Coastal Bermudagrass, fescue, and white clover sod.

The average rates for pan evaporation were highest in May and gradually decreased as the season progressed (fig. 1). Pan evaporation rates varied considerably between 10-day periods and between years.

The average rates of net radiation, assuming a constant value for heat of vaporization, increased from the beginning of the growing season in April, reached a maximum about the last of June, and then decreased for the rest of the season. There was close agreement between the average rates of pan evaporation and net radiation. The general trend during the growing season for the mean air temperature was similar to trends by pan evaporation and net radiation, except the downward trend of temperature began somewhat later than did the trends of pan evaporation and net radiation.

Moisture Use Rates

The rate of moisture use was controlled by meteorological factors and the type and extent of vegetative cover when water was readily available. There were many short periods and a few

TABLE 4.--Average daily mean air temperature by 10-day periods throughout growing season for each year, 1956-62

Period		Year							Average
		1956	1957	1958	1959	1960	1961	1962	
		°F.	°F.	°F.	°F.	°F.	°F.	°F.	°F.
Feb.	11-20	--	45	--	--	--	--	--	--
	21-28	--	46	--	--	--	--	--	--
March	1-10	--	44	--	--	--	--	--	--
	11-20	--	57	--	--	--	--	--	--
	21-31	52	50	51	54	50	60	59	54
April	1-10	59	61	57	63	58	51	54	58
	11-20	55	58	60	57	60	54	56	57
	21-30	64	69	68	62	69	65	61	65
May	1-10	70	62	64	73	60	66	70	66
	11-20	71	71	69	69	63	66	78	70
	21-31	73	72	73	73	73	66	78	73
June	1-10	70	73	78	72	74	75	76	74
	11-20	73	78	77	75	73	70	75	74
	21-30	78	77	73	78	79	70	76	76
July	1-10	77	78	75	77	80	74	78	77
	11-20	77	79	78	75	80	74	80	78
	21-31	78	77	78	78	79	77	79	78
Aug.	1-10	80	78	79	78	78	77	79	78
	11-20	80	79	78	78	76	76	78	78
	21-31	74	74	76	80	76	74	78	76
Sept.	1-10	74	75	76	77	78	77	78	76
	11-20	70	74	73	67	72	67	77	71
	21-30	67	65	72	73	70	74	66	70
Oct.	1-10	67	60	62	74	70	64	70	67
	11-20	64	60	66	63	67	61	70	64
	21-31	60	52	58	56	56	60	56	57

long periods when moisture was limiting on the unirrigated soil moisture regime. Rates of moisture use were affected by the availability of moisture in the soil in the different irrigated treatments.

The average daily moisture use rates for each species throughout the growing season are shown in figures 2 to 5. These 15 species were divided into 4 groups--cultivated crops, warm season perennial forages, cool season perennial legumes, and cool season perennial grasses. These curves were constructed by averaging values of 3- to 5-day periods and represent an average of all years for each moisture regime. They do not reflect the daily fluctuation in weather conditions or effects of clipping the forages. The period of record for each species is given in table 5.

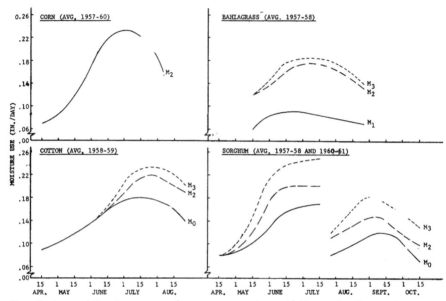

Figure 2.--Average daily moisture-use rate for corn, cotton, sorghum, and bahiagrass throughout growing season.

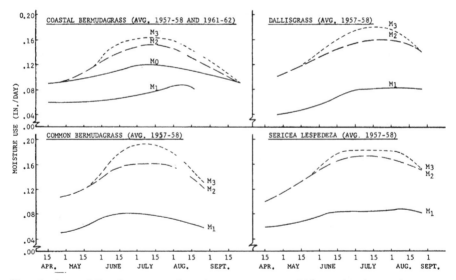

Figure 3.--Average daily moisture-use rate for various warm season perennial forages throughout growing season.

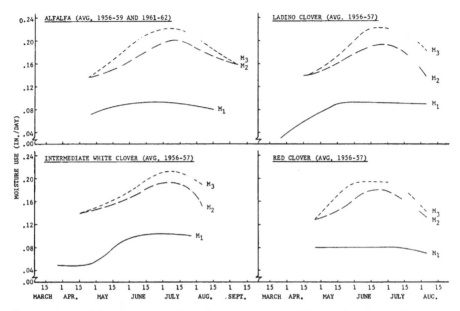

Figure 4.--Average daily moisture-use rate for various cool season perennial legumes throughout growing season.

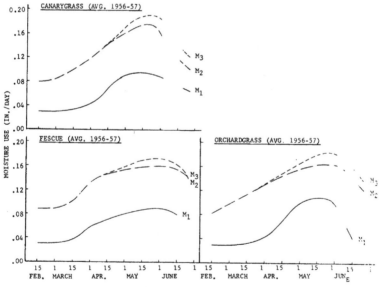

Figure 5.--Average daily moisture-use rate for various cool season perennial grasses throughout growing season.

9

TABLE 5.--Seasonal average rate of moisture use (ET), open pan evaporation (E), net radiation (Rn), ratio of ET/E and ET/Rn, and correlation coefficients of these ratios

Species	Moisture regime	Year	ET	E	Rn	ET/E	ET/Rn	Correlation coefficients	
								ET:E	ET:Rn
			Inches per day						
Corn	M_2	1957	0.18	0.25	0.18	0.71	0.99	0.61	0.77
		1958	.17	.20	.16	.85	1.06	.78	.77
		1959	.19	.19	.16	1.00	1.14	.87	.88
		1960	.15	.21	.17	.73	.89	.79	.84
Cotton	M_0	1958	.15	.19	.15	.77	.99	.88	.88
		1959	.12	.19	.16	.62	.78	.86	.99
	M_2	1958	.16	.19	.15	.85	1.10	.86	.88
		1959	.16	.19	.16	.88	.98	.96	.98
	M_3	1958	.17	.19	.15	.91	1.18	.82	.88
		1959	.19	.19	.16	1.02	1.13	.93	.95
		1960	.18	.19	.16	.92	1.09	.63	.70
		1961	.16	.18	.15	.89	1.07	.92	.95
		1962	.18	.19	.15	.95	1.17	.97	.97
Sorghum	M_0	1957	.10	.18	.13	.57	.79	.69	.72
		1958	.13	.20	.13	.68	1.03	.19	.72
		1960	.10	.17	.14	.60	.72	.58	.68
		1961	.11	.16	.14	.68	.83	.50	.54
	M_2	1957	.16	.18	.13	.89	1.23	.91	.84
		1958	.15	.20	.13	.78	1.18	.21	.80
		1960	.14	.17	.14	.81	.98	.70	.80
		1961	.13	.16	.14	.78	.95	.39	.51
	M_3	1957	.16	.18	.13	.91	1.24	.93	.87
		1958	.18	.20	.13	.91	1.38	.18	.77
		1960	.18	.17	.14	1.03	1.24	.62	.56
		1961	.16	.16	.14	.98	1.19	.32	.42
Bahiagrass	M_1	1957	.08	.20	.16	.38	.46	.90	.75
		1958	.06	.19	.15	.33	.43	.94	.90
	M_2	1957	.14	.20	.16	.70	.35	.91	.97
		1958	.14	.19	.15	.73	.96	.81	.80
	M_3	1957	.15	.20	.16	.73	.89	.95	.92
		1958	.15	.19	.15	.76	1.00	.97	.95
Coastal bermuda-grass	M_0	1961	.10	.17	.14	.58	.71	.68	.83
		1962	.10	.20	.15	.53	.71	.78	.82
	M_1	1957	.08	.21	.16	.36	.46	.75	.63
		1958	.06	.19	.15	.32	.42	.90	.94
	M_2	1957	.14	.21	.16	.69	.87	.84	.74
		1958	.14	.19	.15	.70	.92	.96	.98
		1961	.12	.17	.14	.71	.86	.72	.84
		1962	.12	.20	.15	.61	.83	.89	.93
	M_3	1957	.16	.21	.16	.75	.95	.79	.73
		1958	.15	.19	.15	.78	1.01	.96	.96
		1961	.13	.17	.14	.73	.89	.68	.83
		1962	.13	.20	.15	.64	.86	.91	.94

TABLE 5.--Seasonal average rate of moisture use (ET), open pan evaporation (E), net radiation (Rn), ratio of ET/E and ET/Rn, and correlation coefficients of these ratios--Con.

Species	Moisture regime	Year	ET	E	Rn	ET/E	ET/Rn	Correlation coefficient	
								ET:E	ET:Rn
					Inches per day				
Common bermuda-grass	M_1	1957	0.07	0.21	0.16	0.34	0.42	0.89	0.84
		1958	.06	.19	.14	.31	.41	.98	.98
	M_2	1957	.14	.21	.16	.67	.84	.64	.90
		1958	.14	.19	.14	.73	.97	.97	.98
	M_3	1957	.15	.21	.16	.72	.90	.87	.86
		1958	.15	.19	.14	.78	1.03	.95	.96
Dallisgrass	M_1	1957	.07	.22	.18	.33	.42	.91	.84
		1958	.06	.19	.15	.32	.42	.99	.99
	M_2	1957	.14	.22	.18	.64	.80	.94	.86
		1958	.14	.19	.15	.72	.94	.96	.98
	M_3	1957	.15	.22	.18	.69	.86	.93	.93
		1958	.15	.19	.15	.77	1.01	.95	.97
Lespedeza sericea	M_1	1957	.08	.22	.18	.38	.47	.92	.87
		1958	.07	.19	.15	.34	.45	.98	.97
	M_2	1957	.15	.22	.18	.70	.87	.94	.87
		1958	.14	.19	.15	.76	.99	.99	.99
	M_3	1957	.17	.22	.18	.79	.98	.95	.92
		1958	.15	.19	.15	.78	1.01	.99	.99
Alfalfa	M_1	1956	.10	.21	--	.48	--	.93	--
		1957	.07	.22	.17	.30	.38	.95	.92
	M_2	1956	.16	.21	--	.78	--	.95	--
		1957	.16	.22	.17	.74	.92	.97	.94
		1961	.16	.17	.15	.91	1.09	.80	.83
		1962	.18	.20	.16	.91	1.18	.90	.95
	M_3	1956	.19	.21	--	.92	--	.90	--
		1957	.16	.22	.17	.75	.94	.96	.94
		1958	.20	.18	.15	1.12	1.33	.88	.94
		1959	.18	.18	.15	.98	1.17	.78	.77
Intermediate white clover	M_1	1956	.09	.22	--	.43	--	.96	--
		1957	.07	.20	.15	.34	.45	.90	.92
	M_2	1956	.16	.22	--	.73	--	.72	--
		1957	.15	.20	.15	.76	1.01	.80	.74
	M_3	1956	.19	.22	--	.88	--	.98	--
		1957	.17	.20	.15	.83	1.11	.94	.88
Ladino clover	M_1	1956	.09	.22	--	.43	--	.95	--
		1957	.07	.20	.15	.36	.47	.94	.92
	M_2	1956	.16	.22	--	.75	--	.96	--
		1957	.16	.20	.15	.81	1.08	.79	.68
	M_3	1956	.20	.22	--	.91	--	.92	--
		1957	.17	.20	.15	.86	1.15	.97	.88
Red clover	M_1	1956	.10	.22	--	.44	--	.94	--
		1957	.06	.22	.17	.28	.34	.97	.96
	M_2	1956	.15	.22	--	.71	--	.95	--
		1957	.14	.22	.17	.63	.80	.90	.89
	M_3	1956	.18	.22	--	.81	--	.93	--
		1957	.17	.22	.17	.79	.99	.96	.94

11

TABLE 5.--Seasonal average rate of moisture use (ET) 'open pan evaporation (E), net radiation (Rn), ratio of ET/E and ET/Rn, and correlation coefficients of these ratios--Con.

Species	Moisture regime	Year	ET	E	Rn	ET/E	ET/Rn	Correlation coefficient	
								ET:E	ET:Rn
					Inches per day				
Canarygrass	M_1	1956	0.09	0.21	--	0.44	--	0.90	--
		1957	.06	.15	.12	.37	.55	.89	.87
	M_2	1956	.12	.21	--	.59	--	.73	.--
		1957	.14	.15	.12	.97	1.36	.71	.92
	M_3	1956	.16	.21	--	.76	--	.80	--
		1957	.16	.15	.12	1.09	1.60	.86	.82
Fescue	M_1	1956	.08	.21	--	.39	--	.91	--
		1957	.05	.15	.12	.36	.52	.95	.82
	M_2	1956	.15	.21	--	.70	--	.80	--
		1957	.13	.15	.12	.86	1.18	.84	.71
	M_3	1956	.17	.21	--	.82	--	.73	--
		1957	.14	.15	.12	.92	1.28	.94	.81
Orchardgrass	M_1	1956	.08	.21	--	.37	--	.82	--
		1957	.06	.15	.12	.42	.62	.88	.88
	M_2	1956	.14	.21	--	.68	--	.95	--
		1957	.14	.15	.12	.94	1.34	.89	.80
	M_3	1956	.16	.21	--	.77	--	.72	--
		1957	.14	.15	.12	.94	1.34	.90	.85

The average daily moisture-use rates ranged from 0.03 to 0.24 inch, depending on season of year, soil moisture regime, stage of plant growth, and species (figs. 2, 3, 4, and 5). The rates were low during the first part of the growing season and gradually increased until a peak-use rate was reached during periods when both solar energy and vegetative growth rates were high. The peak reached was in proportion to the amount of water available. After the peak-use rate was reached, the average rates usually decreased as the season progressed.

The average moisture-use rates for cultivated crops usually reached a maximum in July. Warm season forage species usually reached a maximum-use rate in June or July, whereas the cool season forages had the highest use rate in May. The daily moisture-use rates for the sod species were usually lower immediately after clipping and increased to maximum rates immediately before the next clipping. Also, moisture-use rates were generally higher shortly after irrigation than immediately before, depending to some extent on stage of plant growth.

There was little difference in maximum moisture-use rates between the cotton, corn, and sorghum for corresponding moisture regimes. Average daily rates were 0.08 to 0.10 inch early in the spring and reached a maximum of 0.18, 0.22, and 0.24 inch, respectively, for the M_0, M_2, and M_3 moisture regimes.

Average daily rates within a season for all warm season perennial forage species ranged from 0.06 to 0.18 inch, with little difference in average rates for a given period between the different species. Average daily rates for the cool season perennial legume species ranged from 0.06 to 0.21 inch, with maximum rates slightly higher than for the warm season perennial forages (figs. 3 and 4). Rates for alfalfa and red clover were slightly higher than rates for intermediate white and ladino clovers. This was probably due to a deeper root system for alfalfa and red clover (2). Average daily rates were usually lower for the cool season perennial grasses than for the cool season legume species. Rates ranged from 0.03 inch per day early in the season to 0.18 inch during the peak moisture-use period. There was little difference in average rates for fescue and canarygrass, with orchardgrass rates being slightly lower than these.

All species first extracted soil moisture in the upper portion of the soil where root concentrations were highest and then at successively lower depths as the moisture supply was depleted. The rate of water removal at the lower depths was not sufficient to supply the plants with adequate moisture for normal transpiration. Root samples taken from each warm and cool season perennial forage species at all moisture regimes after the study was completed showed that more than 75 percent of the roots of all species was found in the top 12 inches of soil and that soil moisture extractions were a good indication of the effective rooting depth (2,7). This indicates the moisture in the upper foot of this soil is the most important for practical irrigation purposes.

Relation of ET to E

The average ratio of moisture use to open pan evaporation throughout the growing season is shown in figure 6 for cotton, Coastal bermudagrass, alfalfa, and fescue. These four species represent the four groups--cultivated crops, warm season perennial forages, cool season perennial legumes, and cool season perennial grasses. There was little difference in ratios of different species within a group. Ratios for all species depended on meteorological factors, the amount of vegetative growth, and soil moisture regime. The ratios of ET/E for the cool season grasses (canarygrass, fescue, and orchardgrass) increased only slightly from the beginning of the growing season in early spring and reached a maximum in April or May. The ratios for the warm season crops were lowest during the early spring, gradually increased with plant growth until a maximum was reached in June or July, and then decreased for the remainder of the growing season. The general relationship and shapes of these curves (fig. 6) are similar to those presented by others for corn (5,6,8).

Relation of ET to Rn

The average ratios of moisture use to net radiation throughout the growing season are shown in figure 7 for cotton, Coastal bermudagrass, alfalfa, and fescue, which represent the four species groups. The general shape of these curves is similar to those for ratio of ET/E for the cotton, Coastal bermudagrass, and fescue. Ratios for these crops were usually lowest in the first part of the growing season, increased as stage of growth and season progressed, and reached a peak usually when maximum vegetative growth was obtained. Ratios of ET/Rn for alfalfa declined steadily from late April to early August.

Figure 7 shows that moisture-use rates by most species under irrigation exceeded the equivalent of net radiation during part of the growing season. This could have been the result of advective heat transfer since the irrigated plots were relatively small and a large amount of the surrounding area was not irrigated or of the fact that deep percolation losses were not fully accounted for. The net radiation equivalent rates used were for the total 24-hour period each day. Net radiation was always negative during the nighttime. The rates would have been considerably higher if only the daytime period had been used and thus the ratios of ET/Rn would have been lower. Ratios of ET/Rn greater than 1.0 have been reported by others (13).

The curves in figures 6 and 7 give the general trend of ET/E and ET/Rn during the growing season as determined by average values for the period of record. Records for the individual periods of measurements usually showed a series of high peaks followed by declining values, because the ratios were highest immediately after irrigation or rain and declined as the available soil moisture was depleted. Ratios of both ET/E and ET/Rn for all species were lower when the soil was dry than when it was wet. This agrees with previous reports for the ratio of ET/Rn (9, 11).

13

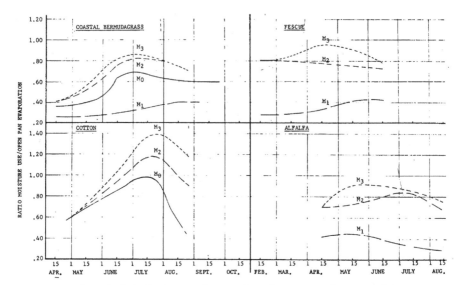

Figure 6.--Ratio of moisture use by Coastal bermudagrass, cotton, fescue, and alfalfa to open pan evaporation throughout growing season.

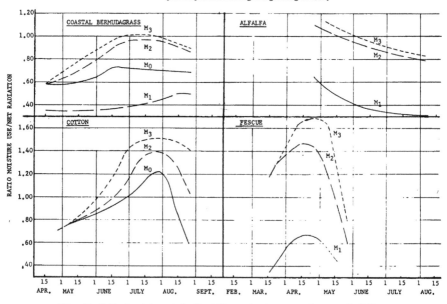

Figure 7.--Ratio of moisture use by Coastal bermudagrass, cotton, fescue, and alfalfa to net radiation throughout growing season.

14

Correlation Between ET/E and ET/Rn

There was a high degree of correlation between moisture use and pan evaporation during the entire growing season in all cases except for sorghum during 1958 at all moisture regimes and at the M_3 regime in 1961 (table 5). Moisture use and net radiation also were correlated except for sorghum M3 in 1961 (table 5). Correlations were made on basis of the actual 3- to 5-day measurement periods. Correlation coefficients were greater for sorghum after the plants reached a height of 12 inches. Lower correlations of moisture use by sorghum to pan evaporation and net radiation (values measured over sod crops) were probably due to (1) the net radiometer readings taken over sod crops and thus not necessarily accurate measurements of the energy levels over the row crops, particularly during the early growth period; and (2) two crops of sorghum that were grown each season, with the first crop harvested the last of July during the peak energy and moisture-use period and the second crop planted in early August after the energy began to decline.

Estimating Daily Moisture Use

Daily moisture-use rates can be estimated from records of open pan evaporation or net radiation if the relations between moisture use and pan evaporation or net radiation have been established. Recorded values of pan evaporation or net radiation can be multiplied by the appropriate ratio of ET/E or ET/Rn to obtain moisture use values corresponding to a given crop, stage of growth, and soil moisture regime.

SUMMARY

Moisture use rates by 15 plant species were determined on a Greenville fine sandy loam soil at Thorsby, Ala., during 1956 to 1962. Average daily moisture-use rates (ET) ranged from 0.03 to 0.24 inch, depending on season of year, available soil moisture, stage of plant growth, and species. In general, moisture-use rates were highest for cultivated crops and lowest for cool season perennial grasses. Moisture-use rates of species with similar seasonal growth characteristics differed little within a group, i.e., cultivated crops, warm season perennial forages, cool season perennial legumes, and cool season perennial grasses.

Moisture-use rates for 10-day periods determined from gravimetric soil sampling at 3- to 5-day intervals throughout the growing season for each species at each soil moisture regime were correlated separately with open pan evaporation and the inches of moisture equivalent of net radiation, assuming a constant value for heat of vaporization. These relations indicate that either open pan evaporation or net radiation may be used to estimate moisture use under conditions where moisture is not limiting, provided a relation has been established for the given species. To estimate moisture use on a daily basis, the appropriate ET/E or ET/Rn ratio is multiplied by the measured daily pan evaporation or inches moisture equivalent of net radiation.

LITERATURE CITED

(1) Ashcroft, G., and Taylor, S. A.
    1953. Soil moisture tensions as a measure of water removal rate from soil, and its relation to weather factors. Soil Sci. Soc. Amer. Proc. 17: 171-174.
(2) Bennett, O. L., and Doss, B. D.
    1960. Effect of soil moisture level on root distribution of cool-season forage species. Agron. Jour. 52: 204-207.

(3) Blaney, H. F.
    1955. Climate as an index of irrigation needs. U.S. Dept. Agr. Yearbook 1955: 341-345, illus.

(4)_____ and Criddle, W. D.
    1962. Determining consumptive use and irrigation water requirements. U.S. Dept. Agr. Tech. Bul. 1275, 59 pp.

(5) Denmead, O. T., and Shaw, R. H.
    1959. Evapotranspiration in relation to the development of the corn crop. Agron. Jour. 51: 725-726.

(6) Doss, B. D., Bennett, O. L., and Ashley, D. A.
    1962. Evapotranspiration by irrigated corn. Agron. Jour. 54: 497-498.

(7)_____ Ashley, D. A., and Bennett, O. L.
    1960. Effect of soil moisture regime on root distribution of warm season forage species. Agron. Jour. 52: 569-572.

(8) Fritschen, L. J., and Shaw, R. H.
    1961. Evapotranspiration for corn as related to pan evaporation. Agron. Jour. 53: 149-150.

(9) Gerber, J. F., and Decker, W. L.
    1960. A comparison of evapotranspiration as estimated by the heat budget and measured by the water balance from a corn field. Mo. Univ. Final Rpt. USWB Contract Cwb-9563.

(10) Graham, W. G., and King, K. M.
    1961. Fraction of net radiation utilized in evapotranspiration from a corn crop. Soil Sci. Soc. Amer. Proc. 25: 158-160.

(11) Halstead, M. H.
    1954. The fluxes of momentum, heat and water vapor in micro-meteorology. The Johns Hopkins Univ., Pub. in Climatology 7: 326-361.

(12) Jensen, M. C., Middleton, J. E., and Pruitt, W. O.
    1961. Scheduling irrigation from pan evaporation. Wash. Agr. Expt. Sta. Cir. 386, pp. 1-14.

(13) Lemon E. R., Glaser, A. H., and Satterwhite, L. E.
    1957. Some aspects of the relationship of soil, plant, and meteorological factors to evapotranspiration. Soil Sci. Soc. Amer. Proc. 21: 464-468.

(14) Penman, H. L.
    1948. Natural evaporation from open water, bare soil, and grass. Roy. Soc. London Proc. 193: 120-145.

(15)_____
    1952. Experiments on irrigation of sugar beets. Jour. Agr. Sci. 42 (3): 286-292.

(16) Thornthwaite, C. W.
    1948. An approach toward a rational classification of climate. Geog. Rev. 38: 55-94.

CPSIA information can be obtained
at www.ICGtesting.com
Printed in the USA
BVHW08s1102170918
527713BV00021B/583/P